Fast&Fresh!

Quick, easy and tasty recipes for every day

pil

Publications International, Ltd.

Photograph on front cover and page 41 copyright © Shutterstock.com.

Pictured on the front cover: Chicken and Watercress Wraps *(page 40)*.

Pictured on the back cover *(left to right):* Turkey Taco Bowls *(page 118)* and Greek Salad *(page 69)*.

ISBN: 978-1-63938-054-1

Manufactured in China.

8 7 6 5 4 3 2 1

Microwave Cooking: Microwave ovens vary in wattage. Use the cooking times as guidelines and check for doneness before adding more time.

WARNING: Food preparation, baking and cooking involve inherent dangers: misuse of electric products, sharp electric tools, boiling water, hot stoves, allergic reactions, foodborne illnesses and the like, pose numerous potential risks. Publications International, Ltd. (PIL) assumes no responsibility or liability for any damages you may experience as a result of following recipes, instructions, tips or advice in this publication.

While we hope this publication helps you find new ways to eat delicious foods, you may not always achieve the results desired due to variations in ingredients, cooking temperatures, typos, errors, omissions or individual cooking abilities.

Let's get social!

 @Publications_International

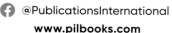 @PublicationsInternational

www.pilbooks.com

Contents

Smart Starts

Extra Green Avocado Toast

— makes 2 servings —

½ cup thawed frozen peas

2 teaspoons lemon juice

1 teaspoon minced fresh tarragon

¼ teaspoon salt

⅛ teaspoon black pepper

4 slices hearty whole grain bread, toasted

1 avocado

1 tablespoon toasted pumpkin seeds

1 Combine peas, lemon juice, tarragon, salt and pepper in small food processor; pulse until blended but still chunky. (Or combine ingredients in small bowl and mash with fork to desired consistency.)

2 Spread about 1 tablespoon pea mixture over each slice of bread.

3 Cut avocado in half lengthwise around pit. Cut avocado into slices in shell; use spoon to scoop out slices. Arrange slices over pea mixture; top with pumpkin seeds.

Effortless Oatmeal >>

—————— makes 2 servings ——————

1¾ cups water

⅓ cup old-fashioned oats

⅓ cup oat bran

1 tablespoon packed brown sugar

¼ teaspoon ground cinnamon

⅛ teaspoon salt

½ cup fresh blueberries

1 Combine water, oats, oat bran, brown sugar, cinnamon and salt in large microwavable bowl; mix well.

2 Cover with vented plastic wrap; microwave on HIGH about 6 minutes or until thickened. Stir oatmeal; let stand 2 minutes before serving. Top with blueberries.

Lighter Breakfast Sandwiches

—————— makes 4 servings ——————

3 eggs

¼ teaspoon salt

¼ teaspoon black pepper *or*
    ⅛ teaspoon hot pepper sauce

3 slices (2 ounces) Canadian
    bacon, chopped

1 green onion, thinly sliced

2 teaspoons butter

⅓ cup shredded sharp Cheddar
    cheese

4 multigrain English muffins,
    split and toasted

1 Whisk eggs, salt and pepper in medium bowl until blended. Stir in Canadian bacon and green onion.

2 Heat butter in medium nonstick skillet over medium-high heat until bubbly. Add egg mixture; cook 2 to 3 minutes or until eggs are soft-set, stirring frequently. Remove from heat; stir in cheese. Serve on English muffins.

Banana Chai Smoothie >>

—————— makes 2 servings ——————

¾ cup water

¼ cup coconut milk

2 frozen bananas

1 teaspoon honey

¼ teaspoon ground ginger

¼ teaspoon ground cinnamon

¼ teaspoon vanilla

Pinch ground cloves

Combine water, coconut milk, bananas, honey, ginger, cinnamon, vanilla and cloves in blender; blend until smooth. Serve immediately.

Super C Smoothie

—————— makes 3 servings ——————

⅔ cup water

2 navel oranges, peeled and seeded

2 cups frozen blackberries

2 cups baby kale

1 avocado

2 tablespoons honey

Combine water, oranges, blackberries, kale, avocado and honey in blender; blend until smooth. Serve immediately.

Greek Isles Omelet

———— makes 2 servings ————

1 tablespoon olive oil, divided

¼ cup chopped onion

¼ cup canned artichoke hearts, drained and sliced

¼ cup chopped fresh spinach

¼ cup chopped plum tomato

2 tablespoons sliced pitted black olives, rinsed and drained

4 eggs

¼ teaspoon salt

Dash black pepper

1 Heat half of oil in small nonstick skillet over medium heat. Add onion; cook and stir 2 minutes or until crisp-tender. Add artichokes; cook and stir until heated through. Gently stir in spinach, tomato and olives; cook 1 minute. Remove to small bowl.

2 Wipe out skillet with paper towels; add remaining oil and heat over medium heat. Whisk eggs, salt and and pepper in medium bowl until well blended. Pour into skillet; cook and stir gently, lifting edge to allow uncooked portion to flow underneath. Cook just until set.

3 Spoon vegetable mixture over half of omelet. Gently loosen omelet with spatula and fold in half. Cut in half; serve immediately.

Cherry Pie Oatmeal >>

———————— makes 4 servings ————————

4 cups water

3 cups old-fashioned oats

⅔ cup nonfat dry milk powder

½ cup dried cherries

¼ cup packed dark brown sugar

½ teaspoon salt

Milk (optional)

1 Bring water to a boil in large saucepan over high heat. Stir in oats, milk powder, cherries, brown sugar and salt; mix well.

2 Reduce heat to medium-high; cook 4 to 5 minutes or until thick and creamy, stirring frequently. Serve with milk, if desired.

Egg-Stuffed Tomatoes

———————— makes 4 servings ————————

4 medium tomatoes

¼ cup grated Parmesan cheese

4 eggs

4 teaspoons minced green onion

Salt and black pepper

1 Preheat oven to 375°F. Cut thin slice off bottom of each tomato so they lay flat. Sccop out and discard seeds and pulp. Place tomatoes in shallow baking dish.

2 Sprinkle 1 tablespoon cheese inside each tomato. Break 1 egg into each tomato; top with green onion, salt and pepper.

3 Bake 15 to 20 minutes or until eggs are set.

Mexican Breakfast Burrito

—————— makes 4 servings ——————

8 eggs

¼ teaspoon salt

⅛ teaspoon black pepper

2 teaspoons vegetable oil

⅓ cup canned black beans,
   rinsed and drained

2 tablespoons sliced green onions

2 (10-inch) flour tortillas

¼ cup shredded Cheddar cheese

¼ cup salsa

1 Whisk eggs, salt and pepper in medium bowl until blended. Heat oil in large nonstick skillet over medium heat. Pour egg mixture into skillet; cook 5 to 7 minutes or until mixture begins to set, stirring occasionally.

2 Stir in beans and green onions; cook 3 minutes or just until eggs are cooked through, stirring frequently.

3 Spoon mixture evenly down centers of tortillas; top with cheese. Roll up to enclose filling. Cut in half; top with salsa.

Blueberry Banana Oatmeal Smoothie >>

———— makes 2 servings ————

1 cup milk

1 small ripe banana

½ cup frozen blueberries

½ cup plain yogurt

¼ cup quick oats

Combine milk, banana and blueberries in blender; blend until smooth. Add yogurt and oats; blend until smooth. Serve immediately.

Green Islander Smoothie

———— makes 2 servings ————

2 cups ice cubes

1 banana

1 cup fresh pineapple chunks

1 cup packed stemmed spinach

1 cup packed stemmed kale

Combine ice, banana, pineapple, spinach and kale in blender; blend until smooth. Serve immediately.

Harvest Apple Oatmeal >>

—————— makes 1 serving ——————

1 cup water

½ cup old-fashioned oats

½ cup chopped Granny Smith apple

2 tablespoons raisins

1 teaspoon packed brown sugar

¼ teaspoon ground cinnamon

⅛ teaspoon salt

1 Combine water, oats, apple, raisins, brown sugar, cinnamon and salt in large microwavable mug or medium bowl; mix well.

2 Microwave on HIGH 1½ minutes. Stir oatmeal; microwave on HIGH 1 minute or until thickened and liquid is absorbed. Let stand 1 to 2 minutes before serving.

Smoked Salmon Scramble

—————— makes 4 servings ——————

8 eggs

¼ teaspoon salt

⅛ teaspoon black pepper

2 teaspoons olive oil

2 ounces smoked salmon, flaked

2 tablespoons sliced green onion

1 ounce cold cream cheese,
    cut into ¼-inch cubes

1 Whisk eggs, salt and pepper in medium bowl until blended. Heat oil in large nonstick skillet over medium heat. Pour egg mixture into skillet; cook 5 to 7 minutes or until mixture begins to set, stirring occasionally.

2 Gently fold in salmon, green onion and cream cheese; cook about 3 minutes or just until eggs are cooked through but are still slightly moist, stirring occaionally.

Zucchini Omelet with Dill

makes 2 servings

5 eggs
2 tablespoons milk
½ teaspoon dried dill weed
⅛ teaspoon salt

⅛ teaspoon black pepper
1 tablespoon butter
1 cup diced zucchini

1 Whisk eggs, milk, dill, salt and pepper in medium bowl until well blended.

2 Melt butter in medium nonstick skillet over medium-high heat. Add zucchini; cook 4 minutes or until lightly browned, stirring occasionally.

3 Add egg mixture to skillet; cook until edges are set. Push edges toward center with spatula; tilt skillet to allow uncooked portion to flow underneath. When eggs are set, fold omelet over and cut in half.

Berry Morning Medley >>

———— makes 2 servings ————

1 cup frozen mixed berries

1½ cups milk

½ cup plain yogurt

1 tablespoon sugar

¼ teaspoon vanilla

¼ cup granola, plus additional
for garnish

Combine berries and milk in blender; blend until thick and creamy. Add yogurt, sugar and vanilla; blend until smooth. Add ¼ cup granola; pulse 15 to 20 seconds. Sprinkle with additional granola, if desired.

Rise 'n' Shine Smoothie

———— makes 2 servings ————

½ cup uncooked old-fashioned
oats

1 cup orange juice

6 ounces vanilla yogurt

½ cup milk

4 whole strawberries

3 ice cubes

1 teaspoon ground cinnamon

1 Pour oats into blender; blend into fine crumbs.

2 Add orange juice, yogurt, milk, strawberries, ice and cinnamon to blender; blend until smooth. Serve immediately.

Scrambled Egg and Roasted Pepper Pockets

—— makes 1 serving ——

2 eggs

1 tablespoon milk

⅛ teaspoon salt

⅛ teaspoon black pepper

2 teaspoons butter, softened, divided

3 tablespoons minced red onion

2 tablespoons diced roasted red pepper (blot before dicing)

1 whole wheat pita bread round, cut in half crosswise

1 Whisk eggs, milk, salt and black pepper in small bowl until well blended.

2 Heat 1 teaspoon butter in medium nonstick skillet over medium heat. Add onion; cook and stir 3 to 5 minutes or until lightly browned. Pour egg mixture into skillet; sprinkle with roasted pepper. Stir gently, lifting edge to allow uncooked portion to flow underneath. Cook just until set.

3 Spread inside of pita halves with remaining 1 teaspoon butter. Spoon egg mixture into pita halves.

Wrap it Up

Spinach Veggie Wrap

— makes 4 servings —

1 cup guacamole (purchased or homemade; see page 93)

4 (10-inch) whole wheat tortillas

2 cups fresh baby spinach

1 cup sliced mushrooms

1 cup shredded Asiago cheese

1 cup pico de gallo

Salsa (optional)

1 Spread ¼ cup guacamole on each tortilla. Layer with ½ cup spinach, ¼ cup mushrooms, ¼ cup cheese and ¼ cup pico de gallo.

2 Roll up tortillas to enclose filling. Cut wraps into halves diagonally. Serve with salsa, if desired.

— *Tip* —

Fresh pico de gallo can be found in plastic containers in the refrigerated section of the supermarket (along with guacamole, hummus and other dips), or in jars in the salsa aisle. To make your own pico de gallo, combine 1 cup finely chopped tomatoes, ¼ cup chopped white onion, 2 tablespoons minced jalapeño pepper, 2 tablespoons chopped fresh cilantro, 1 teaspoon lime juice and ½ teaspoon salt.

Grilled Buffalo Chicken Wraps

———— makes 4 servings ————

4 boneless skinless chicken breasts
(about 4 ounces each)

¼ cup plus 2 tablespoons buffalo
wing sauce, divided

2 cups broccoli slaw mix

1 tablespoon blue cheese dressing

4 (8-inch) whole wheat tortillas,
warmed

1 Place chicken in large resealable food storage bag. Add ¼ cup buffalo sauce; seal bag and turn to coat. Marinate in refrigerator 15 minutes.

2 Meanwhile, prepare grill for direct cooking or preheat broiler. Grill chicken over medium-high heat 5 to 6 minutes per side or until no longer pink. Remove to cutting board; cool 5 minutes.

3 Slice chicken; place in medium bowl. Add remaining 2 tablespoons buffalo sauce; toss to coat.

4 Combine broccoli slaw and blue cheese dressing in separate medium bowl; mix well.

5 Layer chicken down center third of each tortilla; top with broccoli slaw. Roll up tortillas to enclose filling. Cut wraps into halves diagonally.

———— *Variation* ————
If you don't like the spicy flavor of buffalo wing sauce,
substitute your favorite barbecue sauce.

Turkey Lettuce Wraps
—— makes 12 wraps (about 4 servings) ——

1 teaspoon dark sesame oil

1 pound ground turkey

½ cup sliced green onions

2 tablespoons minced fresh ginger

1 can (8 ounces) water chestnuts, chopped

1 teaspoon soy sauce

¼ cup chopped fresh cilantro

12 large lettuce leaves

Chopped fresh mint and/or chopped peanuts (optional)

1 Heat oil in large skillet over medium-high heat. Add turkey, green onions and ginger; cook 6 to 8 minutes, stirring to break up meat.

2 Add water chestnuts and soy sauce to skillet; cook 3 minutes or until turkey is no longer pink. Remove from heat; stir in cilantro.

3 Spoon about ¼ cup turkey mixture onto each lettuce leaf. Top with chopped mint and/or peanuts, if desired. Roll up to enclose filling.

—— *Variations* ——

Use the turkey mixture as a salad topping or substitute corn tortillas for the lettuce leaves.

Baja Burritos

—— makes 4 servings ——

6 tablespoons vegetable oil, divided

3 tablespoons lime juice, divided

2 teaspoons chili powder

1½ teaspoons lemon-pepper seasoning

1 pound tilapia fillets

3 cups shredded coleslaw mix

½ cup chopped fresh cilantro

¼ teaspoon salt

¼ teaspoon black pepper

Guacamole and pico de gallo (optional)

4 (7-inch) flour tortillas

Lime wedges (optional)

1 Prepare grill for direct cooking or preheat broiler. Combine 2 tablespoons oil, 1 tablespoon lime juice, chili powder and lemon-pepper in large resealable food storage bag. Add fish; seal bag and turn to coat. Let stand at room temperature 10 minutes.

2 Brush grid with 2 tablespoons oil. Remove fish from marinade; discard marinade. Grill fish over medium-high heat, covered, 3 to 4 minutes per side or until center is opaque. (To broil, place 4 inches away from heat source. Broil 3 to 5 minutes per side or until center is opaque.)

3 Combine coleslaw mix, remaining 2 tablespoons oil, 2 tablespoons lime juice, cilantro, salt and pepper in medium bowl; mix well.

4 Layer fish, coleslaw mixture, guacamole and pico de gallo, if desired, on tortillas; roll up tightly into burritos. Serve with additional pico de gallo and lime wedges, if desired.

—— *Tip* ——

Any firm white fish, such as snapper or halibut, can be substituted for the tilapia.

Curried Chicken Wraps

makes 4 servings

⅓ cup mayonnaise

2 tablespoons mango chutney

½ teaspoon curry powder

4 (6-inch) corn or flour tortillas

1½ cups shredded coleslaw mix

1½ cups shredded or chopped
   cooked chicken

2 tablespoons chopped lightly
   salted peanuts

2 tablespoons chopped
   fresh cilantro

1 Combine mayonnaise, chutney and curry powder in small bowl; mix well. Spread mixture evenly over one side of each tortilla.

2 Top with coleslaw mix, chicken, peanuts and cilantro. Roll up tortillas to enclose filling.

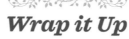
Niçoise Salad Wraps

—————— makes 2 servings ——————

½ cup bite-size green bean pieces

2 new red potatoes, each cut into 8 wedges

3 tablespoons red wine vinaigrette, divided

1 egg

2 cups watercress leaves

4 ounces water-packed albacore tuna, drained and flaked (about ½ cup)

8 niçoise olives, pitted and halved

4 cherry tomatoes, quartered

2 (10-inch) whole wheat tortillas, warmed

1 Bring 8 cups water to a boil in large saucepan over high heat. Add green beans and potatoes. Reduce heat to low; cook 6 minutes or until vegetables are tender. Remove vegetables with slotted spoon to bowl of ice water to stop cooking; drain on paper towels. Transfer to medium bowl; toss with half of vinaigrette.

2 Bring water back to a boil. Add egg; reduce heat to low and cook 12 minutes. Remove to bowl of ice water. When cool enough to handle, peel egg and cut into 8 wedges.

3 Add watercress, tuna, olives, tomatoes and remaining half of vinaigrette to bowl with vegetables; toss gently.

4 Place tortillas on plates. Divide salad mixture between tortillas; top with egg wedges. Roll up tortillas to enclose filling. Cut wraps into halves diagonally.

Easy Moo Shu Pork

—— makes 2 servings ——

2 teaspoons vegetable oil

8 ounces pork tenderloin, cut into ½-inch strips

4 green onions, cut into ½-inch pieces

1½ cups shredded coleslaw mix

2 tablespoons hoisin sauce or Asian plum sauce

4 (8-inch) flour tortillas, warmed

1 Heat oil in large nonstick skillet over medium-high heat. Add pork and green onions; stir-fry 2 to 3 minutes or until pork is barely pink in center. Stir in coleslaw mix and hoisin sauce.

2 Spoon pork mixture onto tortillas. Roll up tortillas, folding in sides to enclose filling.

Tip

To warm tortillas, stack and wrap loosely in plastic wrap.
Microwave on HIGH 15 to 20 seconds or until warm and pliable.

Chicken and Watercress Wraps

—— makes 4 servings ——

3 tablespoons extra virgin olive oil

3 tablespoons lemon juice

1 clove garlic, minced

½ teaspoon ground cumin

¼ teaspoon salt

⅛ teaspoon black pepper

8 ounces boneless skinless chicken breast, cut into ½-inch strips

3 cups watercress, arugula or baby spinach

2 leaves romaine lettuce, shredded (optional)

½ cup cherry tomatoes, halved

½ small red onion, thinly sliced

4 (10-inch) flour tortillas

1 Whisk oil, lemon juice, garlic, cumin, salt and pepper in large bowl until well blended. Remove 2 tablespoons dressing mixture to medium bowl; add chicken and toss to coat.

2 Cook chicken in large skillet over medium-high heat about 4 minutes or until chicken is lightly browned and cooked through, stirring occasionally.

3 Add watercress, lettuce, if desired, tomatoes and onion to large bowl with dressing; toss gently to coat.

4 Place tortillas on plates. Divide salad mixture among tortillas; top with chicken. Roll up tortillas to enclose filling.

Bean and Pepper Burritos

—————— makes 6 servings ——————

1 tablespoon olive oil

1½ cups diced red, yellow and/or green bell peppers *or* 1 large green bell pepper, diced

½ cup chopped onion

1 can (about 15 ounces) black beans, rinsed and drained

½ cup salsa

1 teaspoon chili powder

½ teaspoon salt

6 (8-inch) flour tortillas, warmed

¾ cup (3 ounces) shredded Cheddar or Mexican cheese blend

½ cup chopped fresh cilantro

1 Heat oil in large nonstick skillet over medium heat. Add bell peppers and onion; cook and stir 3 to 4 minutes or until vegetables begin to soften.

2 Stir in beans, salsa, chili powder and salt; cook 5 to 8 minutes or until vegetables are tender and sauce is thickened, stirring occasionally.

3 Spoon about ⅔ cup bean mixture down center third of each tortilla; top with cheese and cilantro. Roll up tortillas to enclose filling.

Chicken, Hummus and Vegetable Wraps

— makes 4 servings —

¾ cup hummus (regular, roasted red pepper or roasted garlic)

4 (8- to 10-inch) sun-dried tomato or spinach wraps or whole wheat flour tortillas

2 cups chopped cooked chicken breast

Hot pepper sauce (optional)

½ cup shredded carrots

½ cup chopped unpeeled cucumber

½ cup thinly sliced radishes

2 tablespoons chopped fresh mint or basil

1 Spread hummus evenly over wraps. Arrange chicken over hummus; sprinkle with hot pepper sauce, if desired.

2 Layer with carrots, cucumber, radishes and mint. Roll up tortillas tightly to enclose filling. Cut wraps into halves diagonally.

Variation

For an appetizer or snack, cut the wraps into bite-size pieces.

Speedy Sandwiches

Quick Caprese Sandwich

—— makes 4 servings ——

1 baguette (16 ounces), ends trimmed

½ cup balsamic vinaigrette

1 cup loosely packed baby arugula

3 medium tomatoes, cut into ¼-inch slices

1 cup roasted red peppers, patted dry and thinly sliced

12 slices fresh mozzarella (one 8-ounce package)

12 fresh basil leaves

1 Cut baguette into four equal pieces; cut each piece in half horizontally.

2 For each sandwich, drizzle 1 tablespoon vinaigrette over bottom half of bread. Layer with arugula, tomatoes, roasted peppers, cheese, additional arugula and basil. Drizzle with 1 tablespoon dressing; replace top half of bread.

Italian Chicken Panini

———— makes 6 servings ————

6 small portobello mushroom caps (about 6 ounces)

½ cup plus 2 tablespoons balsamic vinaigrette

1 loaf (16 ounces) Italian bread, cut into 12 slices

12 slices provolone cheese

1½ cups chopped cooked chicken

1 jar (12 ounces) roasted red peppers, drained

1 Brush mushrooms with 2 tablespoons vinaigrette. Cook mushrooms in large nonstick skillet over medium-high heat 5 to 7 minutes or until softened. Cut diagonally into ½-inch slices.

2 For each sandwich, top 1 bread slice with 1 cheese slice, ¼ cup chicken, mushrooms, roasted peppers, another cheese slice and another bread slice. Brush outsides of sandwiches with remaining dressing.

3 Preheat grill pan or panini press* on medium heat 5 minutes. Cook sandwiches 2 to 3 minutes per side or until cheese is melted and bread is golden brown, turning once.

*If you don't have a grill pan or panini press, cook sandwiches in large nonstick skillet. Place clean heavy pan on top of sandwiches to weigh them down while cooking.

———— *Tip* ————

A rotisserie chicken will yield just enough chopped chicken for this recipe.

Spicy Vegetable Sandwich

makes 4 servings

½ cup plain hummus

½ jalapeño pepper, seeded and minced

¼ cup minced fresh cilantro

8 slices whole wheat bread

4 leaves lettuce (leaf or Bibb lettuce)

2 tomatoes, thinly sliced

½ cucumber, thinly sliced

½ red onion, thinly sliced

½ cup thinly sliced peppadew peppers

4 tablespoons (1 ounce) crumbled feta cheese

1 Combine hummus, jalapeño and cilantro in small bowl; mix well.

2 Spread about 1 tablespoon hummus mixture on one side of each bread slice. Layer half of bread slices with lettuce, tomatoes, cucumber, onion, peppadew peppers and cheese; top with remaining bread slices. Serve immediately.

Mediterranean Chicken Pitas

—————————— makes 6 servings ——————————

2 tablespoons olive oil, divided

1¼ pounds chicken tenders, cut crosswise in half

1 large tomato, diced

½ small cucumber, halved lengthwise, seeded and sliced

½ cup sweet onion slices (about 1 small)

2 tablespoons cider vinegar

1 tablespoon minced fresh oregano *or* ½ teaspoon dried oregano

2 teaspoons minced fresh mint *or* ¼ teaspoon dried mint

½ teaspoon salt

6 (6-inch) whole wheat pita bread rounds, cut in half crosswise

12 lettuce leaves (optional)

1 Heat 1 tablespoon oil in large nonstick skillet over medium heat. Add chicken; cook and stir 6 to 8 minutes or until lightly browned and cooked through. Let stand 5 minutes to cool slightly.

2 Combine chicken, tomato, cucumber and onion in medium bowl. Add vinegar, remaining 1 tablespoon oil, oregano, mint and salt; toss to coat.

3 Place 1 lettuce leaf in each pita bread half, if desired. Divide chicken mixture evenly among pita halves.

Hearty Veggie Sandwich

—————— makes 4 servings ——————

1 pound cremini mushrooms,
   stemmed and thinly sliced
   (⅛-inch slices)

2 tablespoons olive oil, divided

¾ teaspoon salt, divided

¼ teaspoon black pepper

1 medium zucchini, diced
   (¼-inch pieces, about 2 cups)

3 tablespoons butter, softened

8 slices artisan whole grain bread

¼ cup pesto sauce

¼ cup mayonnaise

2 cups packed baby spinach

4 slices mozzarella cheese

1 Preheat oven to 350°F. Combine mushrooms, 1 tablespoon oil, ½ teaspoon salt and pepper in medium bowl; toss to coat. Spread in single layer on large rimmed baking sheet. Roast 20 minutes or until mushrooms are dark brown and dry, stirring after 10 minutes. Cool on baking sheet.

2 Meanwhile, heat remaining 1 tablespoon oil in large skillet over medium heat. Add zucchini and remaining ¼ teaspoon salt; cook and stir 5 minutes or until zucchini is tender and lightly browned. Remove to medium bowl; wipe out skillet with paper towels.

3 Spread butter on one side of each bread slice. Turn over slices. Spread pesto on four bread slices; spread mayonnaise on remaining four slices. Top pesto-covered slices evenly with mushrooms; layer with spinach, zucchini and cheese. Top with remaining bread slices, mayonnaise side down.

4 Heat same skillet over medium heat. Add sandwiches; cover and cook 2 minutes per side or until bread is toasted, spinach is slightly wilted and cheese is beginning to melt. Serve immediately.

Prosciutto Provolone Sandwiches

— makes 4 servings —

1 loaf (16 ounces) French bread

4 teaspoons whole grain Dijon mustard

4 teaspoons cold butter

2 ounces sliced provolone cheese

4 cups spring greens (4 ounces)

8 ounces prosciutto or other thinly sliced ham

1 Cut bread crosswise into four 6-inch pieces; cut each piece in half horizontally.

2 Spread 1 teaspoon mustard on top halves of bread; spread 1 teaspoon butter on bottom halves. Layer cheese, greens and prosciutto over buttered bread halves. Wrap each sandwich with plastic wrap; refrigerate until ready to serve.

Note

Sandwiches may be prepared one day in advance.
Wrap with plastic wrap and refrigerate until ready to serve.

Spinach and Roasted Pepper Panini

—————————————— makes 4 servings ——————————————

1 loaf (12 ounces) focaccia

1½ cups fresh spinach leaves (about 12 leaves)

1 jar (about 7 ounces) roasted red peppers, drained

4 ounces fontina cheese, thinly sliced

¾ cup thinly sliced red onion

Olive oil

1 Cut focaccia in half horizontally. Layer bottom half with spinach, roasted peppers, cheese and onion. Cover with top half of focaccia.

2 Brush outsides of sandwich lightly with oil. Cut sandwich into four equal pieces.

3 Heat large nonstick skillet over medium heat. Add sandwiches; press down lightly with spatula or weigh down with plate. Cook sandwiches 4 to 5 minutes per side or until cheese melts and bread is golden brown.

Almond Chicken Salad Sandwich

———————— makes 4 servings ————————

¼ cup mayonnaise

¼ cup plain Greek yogurt
   or sour cream

2 tablespoons cider vinegar

1 tablespoon honey

1 teaspoon salt

½ teaspoon black pepper

⅛ teaspoon garlic powder

2 cups chopped cooked chicken

¾ cup halved red grapes

1 large stalk celery, chopped

⅓ cup sliced almonds

   Leaf lettuce

1 tomato, thinly sliced

8 slices sesame semolina or
   country Italian bread

1 Whisk mayonnaise, yogurt, vinegar, honey, salt, pepper and garlic powder in small bowl until well blended.

2 Combine chicken, grapes and celery in medium bowl. Add mayonnaise mixture; stir gently to coat. Cover and refrigerate several hours or overnight. Stir in almonds just before making sandwiches.

3 Place lettuce and tomato slices on four bread slices; top with chicken salad and remaining bread slices. Serve immediately.

Portobello and Fontina Sandwiches

—————————— makes 2 servings ——————————

2 teaspoons olive oil, plus
   additional for brushing

2 large portobello mushrooms,
   stems removed

   Salt and black pepper

2 to 3 tablespoons sun-dried
   tomato pesto

4 slices crusty Italian bread

4 ounces fontina cheese, sliced

¼ cup packed fresh basil leaves

1 Preheat broiler. Line baking sheet with foil.

2 Drizzle 2 teaspoons oil over both sides of mushrooms; season with salt and pepper. Place mushrooms, gill sides up, on prepared baking sheet. Broil 4 minutes per side or until mushrooms are tender. Cut into ¼-inch-thick slices.

3 Spread pesto evenly over two bread slices; layer with mushrooms, cheese and basil. Top with remaining bread slices. Brush outsides of sandwiches lightly with additional oil.

4 Heat large grill pan or skillet over medium heat. Add sandwiches; press down lightly with spatula or weigh down with plate. Cook 5 minutes per side or until cheese is melted and bread is golden brown.

Mediterranean Tuna Sandwiches

— makes 4 servings —

1 can (12 ounces) solid white tuna
packed in water, drained

¼ cup finely chopped red onion

¼ cup mayonnaise

3 tablespoons chopped black
olives, drained

1 tablespoon plus 1 teaspoon
lemon juice

1 tablespoon olive oil

1 tablespoon chopped fresh mint
(optional)

¼ teaspoon black pepper

⅛ teaspoon garlic powder

8 slices whole wheat bread

8 leaves romaine lettuce

8 thin slices tomato

1 Combine tuna, onion, mayonnaise, olives, lemon juice, oil, mint, if desired, pepper and garlic powder, if desired, in large bowl; stir gently to blend.

2 Top each of four bread slices with lettuce, tomato, ⅔ cup tuna mixture and remaining bread slices.

Turkey Mozzarella Panini

—————— makes 4 servings ——————

½ cup balsamic vinaigrette

1 loaf (16 ounces) Italian bread, cut in half lengthwise

6 ounces fresh mozzarella cheese, cut into 12 slices

8 ounces thinly sliced oven-roasted deli turkey

½ cup thinly sliced red onion

1 large tomato, thinly sliced

12 to 16 fresh basil leaves

⅛ teaspoon red pepper flakes

1 Preheat indoor grill or panini press.* Brush vinaigrette evenly over cut sides of bread.

2 Arrange cheese evenly over bottom half of bread; top with turkey, onion, tomato and basil. Sprinkle with red pepper flakes. Cover with top half of bread; press down firmly. Cut into four equal pieces.

3 Place sandwiches on grill; close lid. Cook 5 to 7 minutes or until cheese melts.

*If you don't have an indoor grill or panini press, cook sandwiches in large nonstick skillet. Place clean heavy pan on top of sandwiches to weigh them down while cooking.

Simple Salads

Greek Salad

— makes 6 servings —

Salad

- 3 medium tomatoes, cut into 8 wedges each and seeds removed
- 1 green bell pepper, cut into 1-inch pieces
- ½ English cucumber (8 to 10 inches), quartered lengthwise and sliced crosswise
- ½ red onion, thinly sliced
- ½ cup pitted kalamata olives
- 1 block (8 ounces) feta cheese, cut into ½-inch cubes

Dressing

- 6 tablespoons extra virgin olive oil
- 3 tablespoons red wine vinegar
- 1 to 2 cloves garlic, minced
- ¾ teaspoon dried oregano
- ¾ teaspoon salt
- ¼ teaspoon black pepper

1 For salad, combine tomatoes, bell pepper, cucumber, onion and olives in large bowl. Top with cheese.

2 For dressing, whisk oil, vinegar, garlic, oregano, salt and black pepper in small bowl until well blended. Pour over salad; stir gently to coat.

Chickpea Salad

—— makes 4 servings ——

1 can (about 15 ounces) chickpeas, rinsed and drained

1 stalk celery, chopped

1 dill pickle, chopped (about ½ cup)

¼ cup finely chopped red or yellow onion

⅓ cup mayonnaise

1 teaspoon lemon juice

¼ teaspoon salt

⅛ teaspoon black pepper

Whole grain bread (optional)

Lettuce and tomato slices (optional)

1 Place chickpeas in medium bowl. Coarsely mash with potato masher, leaving some beans whole.

2 Add celery, pickles and onion; stir to blend. Add mayonnaise, lemon juice, salt and pepper; mix well. Serve on bread with lettuce and tomato, if desired.

Tomato Watermelon Salad

makes 4 servings

¼ cup extra virgin olive oil

2 tablespoons lemon juice

½ teaspoon honey

½ teaspoon salt

⅛ teaspoon black pepper

2 large heirloom tomatoes
(about 10 ounces each),
cut into 6 slices each

2 cups cubed watermelon
(about 12 ounces)

¼ cup thinly sliced red onion rings

¼ cup crumbled feta cheese

Fresh chervil or parsley sprigs
(optional)

1 Whisk oil, lemon juice, honey, salt and pepper in small bowl until well blended.

2 Arrange tomato slices on four plates. Top with watermelon and onion; sprinkle with cheese. Drizzle with dressing; garnish with chervil.

Thai-Style Warm Noodle Salad

— makes 4 servings —

8 ounces uncooked angel hair pasta

½ cup chunky peanut butter

¼ cup soy sauce

¼ to ½ teaspoon red pepper flakes

2 green onions, thinly sliced

1 carrot, shredded

1 Cook pasta according to package directions.

2 Meanwhile, combine peanut butter, soy sauce and red pepper flakes in large bowl; whisk until smooth.

3 Drain pasta, reserving 5 tablespoons cooking water. Whisk hot pasta water into peanut butter mixture until smooth. Add pasta to sauce; toss to coat. Stir in green onions and carrot. Serve warm or at room temperature.

Notes
This salad can be prepared a day ahead and served warm or cold—perfect for potlucks, picnics and even lunch boxes. Add cooked chicken, beef, pork or tofu to turn it into a heartier meal.

Middle Eastern Spinach Salad

— makes 4 servings —

¼ cup lemon juice

1 tablespoon extra virgin olive oil

1 tablespoon packed brown sugar

½ teaspoon curry powder

¼ teaspoon salt

1 pound fresh spinach, stemmed

½ cup golden raisins

¼ cup minced red onion

¼ cup thin red onion slices

1 Whisk lemon juice, oil, sugar, curry powder and salt in small bowl until blended.

2 Pat spinach dry with paper towels. Tear into bite-size pieces.

3 Combine spinach, raisins, minced onion and onion slices in large bowl. Add dressing; toss gently to coat.

Tomato Quinoa Salad

—————— makes 4 servings ——————

1 cup uncooked quinoa

2 cups water

¾ teaspoon salt, divided

2 tablespoons extra virgin olive oil

1 tablespoon lemon juice

1 clove garlic, minced

2 cups assorted grape tomatoes
 (red, yellow or a combination),
 halved

¼ cup crumbled feta cheese

¼ cup chopped fresh basil

1 Place quinoa in fine-mesh strainer; rinse well under cold running water. Bring 2 cups water and ¼ teaspoon salt to a boil in small saucepan; stir in quinoa. Reduce heat to low; cover and simmer 10 to 15 minutes or until quinoa is tender and water is absorbed.

2 Meanwhile, whisk oil, lemon juice, garlic and remaining ½ teaspoon salt in large bowl until well blended. Gently stir in tomatoes and quinoa. Cover and refrigerate at least 30 minutes.

3 Stir in cheese just before serving. Top with basil.

Chopped Italian Salad

—— makes 4 to 6 servings ——

10 cups chopped romaine lettuce

⅓ cup chopped red onion

20 slices turkey pepperoni, quartered

1 can (2¼ ounces) sliced black olives, drained

1 can (about 15 ounces) chickpeas, rinsed and drained

⅓ cup balsamic vinaigrette

⅓ cup shredded Parmesan cheese

1 Combine lettuce, red onion, pepperoni, olives and chickpeas in large bowl.

2 Add vinaigrette; toss gently to coat. Sprinkle with cheese.

—— *Tip* ——

A chopped salad is the perfect way to use up any leftovers in your refrigerator, including homemade, canned and jarred ingredients. Add cooked chicken or turkey, chopped bacon, steamed or roasted vegetables, hard-cooked eggs, avocado, marinated artichokes or roasted red peppers—simply chop them into bite-size pieces and increase the amount of dressing as necessary.

Bulgur Salad Niçoise

—————— makes 3 to 4 servings ——————

2 cups water

½ teaspoon salt, divided

1 cup bulgur wheat

1 cup halved cherry tomatoes

1 can (6 ounces) tuna packed in water, drained and flaked

½ cup pitted black niçoise olives*

3 tablespoons finely chopped green onions

1 tablespoon chopped fresh mint (optional)

2½ tablespoons lemon juice

2 tablespoons extra virgin olive oil

⅛ teaspoon black pepper

If you use larger olives, slice or chop as desired.

1 Bring water and ¼ teaspoon salt to a boil in medium saucepan over high heat. Stir in bulgur. Remove from heat; cover and let stand 10 to 15 minutes or until water is absorbed and bulgur is tender. Fluff with fork; set aside to cool completely.

2 Combine bulgur, tomatoes, tuna, olives, green onions and mint, if desired, in large bowl.

3 Whisk lemon juice, oil, remaining ¼ teaspoon salt and pepper in small bowl until blended. Pour over salad; toss gently to coat.

Spring Greens with Blueberries, Walnuts and Feta

makes 4 servings

2 tablespoons olive oil

1½ tablespoons white wine vinegar
   or sherry vinegar

2 teaspoons Dijon mustard

¼ teaspoon salt

¼ teaspoon black pepper

5 cups mixed spring greens
   (5 ounces)

1 cup fresh blueberries

½ cup 2 ounces) crumbled
   feta cheese

¼ cup chopped walnuts or pecans,
   toasted*

*To toast nuts, cook in small skillet over medium-low heat about 5 minutes or until nuts begin to brown, stirring frequently.

1 Whisk oil, vinegar, mustard, salt and pepper in large bowl until well blended.

2 Add greens and blueberries; toss gently to coat. Top with cheese and walnuts. Serve immediately.

Greek Rice Salad

—— makes 2 servings ——

1 cup water	1 tablespoon lemon juice
¾ cup uncooked instant brown rice	1½ teaspoons Greek seasoning
1 cup packed baby spinach	¼ teaspoon salt
⅔ cup quartered cherry tomatoes	⅛ teaspoon black pepper
2 tablespoons extra virgin olive oil	¼ cup pine nuts

1 Bring water to a boil in small saucepan over high heat. Add rice; return to a boil. Reduce heat to low; cover and cook 5 minutes. Remove from heat; let stand 5 minutes. Rinse rice under cold water until cool; drain well.

2 Combine spinach, tomatoes and rice in medium bowl. Whisk oil, lemon juice, Greek seasoning, salt and pepper in small bowl until well blended.

3 Pour dressing over spinach mixture; toss gently to coat. Sprinkle with pine nuts just before serving.

Strawberry Spinach Salad with Poppy Seed Dressing

——— makes 4 servings ———

6 cups baby spinach

8 fresh strawberries, halved

¼ cup chopped pecans, toasted*

¼ cup sliced red onion

½ cup crumbled goat cheese

2 tablespoons extra virgin olive oil

2 tablespoons unseasoned rice
   vinegar or raspberry vinegar

2 teaspoons honey

1 teaspoon ground dry mustard

½ teaspoon poppy seeds

¼ teaspoon salt

⅛ teaspoon black pepper

To toast pecans, cook in small skillet over medium-low heat about 5 minutes or until nuts begin to brown, stirring frequently.

1 Place 1½ cups spinach on each of four plates. Top with strawberries, pecans, onions and cheese.

2 Whisk oil, vinegar, honey, mustard, poppy seeds, salt and pepper in small bowl until well blended. Drizzle dressing over salads.

Cellophane Noodle Salad

—————— makes 4 servings ——————

1 package (about 4 ounces) cellophane* noodles

1 tablespoon peanut or vegetable oil

8 ounces medium or large raw shrimp, peeled and deveined (with tails on)

3 cloves garlic, minced

¼ teaspoon red pepper flakes

½ cup cooked pork strips (optional)

2 tablespoons soy sauce

1 tablespoon lime juice

1 tablespoon rice vinegar

1 tablespoon dark sesame oil

⅓ cup thinly sliced green onions or chopped fresh cilantro

Cellophane noodles, also called bean threads or glass noodles, are available in the Asian section of most supermarkets.

1 Place noodles in medium bowl; cover with warm water. Soak 15 minutes to soften. Drain well; cut into 2-inch pieces.

2 Meanwhile, heat large skillet over medium-high heat. Add peanut oil; heat until hot. Add shrimp, garlic and red pepper flakes; cook and stir 2 minutes. Add pork, if desired, soy sauce, lime juice, vinegar and sesame oil; cook and stir 1 minute.

3 Add noodles; cook and stir 1 minute or until heated through. Serve warm, chilled or at room temperature. Sprinkle with green onions.

Snacks & Sides

Guacamole

—— makes 2 cups ——

2 large ripe avocados
2 teaspoons fresh lime juice
¼ cup finely chopped red onion

2 tablespoons chopped fresh cilantro
½ jalapeño pepper, finely chopped
½ teaspoon salt

1 Cut avocados in half lengthwise around pits; remove pits. Scoop avocados into large bowl; sprinkle with lime juice. Mash to desired consistency with fork or potato masher.

2 Add onion, cilantro, jalapeño and ½ teaspoon salt; stir gently until well blended. Taste and add additional salt, if desired.

Mediterranean Baked Feta
—————— makes 4 to 6 servings ——————

1 block (8 ounces) feta cheese,
   cut crosswise into 4 slices

½ cup grape tomatoes, halved

¼ cup sliced roasted red peppers

¼ cup pitted kalamata olives

⅛ teaspoon dried oregano

   Black pepper

2 tablespoons extra virgin olive oil

1 tablespoon shredded fresh basil

   Pita chips or baguette slices

1 Preheat oven to 400°F.

2 Place cheese in small baking dish; top with tomatoes, roasted peppers and olives. Sprinkle with oregano and season with black pepper; drizzle with oil.

3 Bake 12 minutes or until cheese is soft. Sprinkle with basil. Serve immediately with pita chips.

Green Beans with Garlic-Cilantro Butter

—————————— makes 4 to 6 servings ——————————

1½ pounds green beans, trimmed

3 tablespoons butter

1 red bell pepper, cut into thin strips

½ sweet onion, halved and thinly sliced

2 teaspoons minced garlic

1 teaspoon salt

2 tablespoons chopped fresh cilantro

Black pepper

1 Bring large saucepan of salted water to a boil over medium-high heat. Add beans; cook 6 minutes or until tender. Drain beans.

2 Meanwhile, melt butter in large skillet over medium-high heat. Add bell pepper and onion; cook and stir 3 minutes or until vegetables are tender but not browned. Add garlic; cook and stir 30 seconds.

3 Add beans and salt to skillet; cook and stir 2 minutes or until beans are heated through and coated with butter. Stir in cilantro; season with black pepper.

Bulgur Pilaf with Caramelized Onions and Kale

—————————— makes 4 to 6 servings ——————————

1 tablespoon olive oil

1 small onion, cut into thin wedges

1 clove garlic, minced

2 cups chopped kale

2 cups chicken or vegetable broth

¾ cup medium grain bulgur

½ teaspoon salt

¼ teaspoon black pepper

1 Heat oil in large nonstick skillet over medium heat. Add onion; cook about 8 minutes or until softened and lightly browned, stirring frequently. Add garlic; cook and stir 1 minute. Add kale; cook and stir about 1 minute or until kale is wilted.

2 Stir in broth, bulgur, salt and pepper; bring to a boil. Reduce heat to low; cover and cook 12 minutes or until liquid is absorbed and bulgur is tender.

Szechuan Eggplant

—— makes 4 servings ——

1 pound Asian eggplant or regular eggplant, peeled

2 tablespoons peanut or vegetable oil

2 cloves garlic, minced

¼ teaspoon red pepper flakes *or* ½ teaspoon hot chili oil

¼ cup vegetable broth

¼ cup hoisin sauce

3 green onions, cut into 1-inch pieces

Toasted sesame seeds (optional)

1 Cut eggplant into ½-inch slices; cut each slice into ½×½-inch strips.

2 Heat large nonstick skillet over medium-high heat. Add peanut oil; heat until hot. Add eggplant, garlic and red pepper flakes; cook and stir 7 minutes or until eggplant is very tender and browned.

3 Reduce heat to medium. Add broth, hoisin sauce and green onions to skillet; cook and stir 2 minutes. Sprinkle with sesame seeds, if desired.

Classic Tomato Bruschetta

—————— makes 4 servings ——————

1 tablespoon olive oil

1 small clove garlic, minced

2 cups chopped seeded tomatoes
  (about 3 medium)

⅛ teaspoon salt

Black pepper

Toasted Italian bread slices

1 Heat oil and garlic in small skillet over medium heat 2 minutes, stirring occasionally. Remove from heat. Stir in tomatoes, salt and pepper; mix well.

2 Top bread slices with tomato mixture. Serve immediately.

—————— *Variations* ——————

Add 2 tablespoons slivered fresh basil to the tomato mixture in step 1 or sprinkle the basil on top. Top bruschetta with shaved Asiago or Parmesan cheese.

Sautéed Swiss Chard

—————— makes 4 servings ——————

1 large bunch Swiss chard or kale (about 1 pound)

1 tablespoon olive oil

3 cloves garlic, minced

¾ teaspoon salt

¼ teaspoon black pepper

1 tablespoon balsamic vinegar (optional)

¼ cup pine nuts, toasted*

*To toast pine nuts, cook and stir in small skillet over medium heat 1 to 2 minutes or until lightly browned, stirring frequently.

1 Rinse chard in cold water; shake off excess water but do not dry. Finely chop stems and coarsely chop leaves.

2 Heat oil in large saucepan over medium heat. Add garlic; cook and stir 2 minutes. Add chard, salt and pepper; cover and cook 2 minutes or until chard begins to wilt. Uncover; cook and stir about 5 minutes or until chard is softened.

3 Stir in vinegar, if desired. Sprinkle with pine nuts just before serving.

Roasted Cremini Mushrooms

———————— makes 4 servings ————————

1 pound cremini mushrooms, halved

½ cup sliced shallots

1 tablespoon olive oil

½ teaspoon coarse salt

½ teaspoon dried rosemary

¼ teaspoon black pepper

1 Preheat oven to 400°F.

2 Spread mushrooms and shallots on rimmed baking sheet. Whisk oil, salt, rosemary and pepper in small bowl until blended. Drizzle over mushrooms and shallots; toss to coat. Arrange vegetables in single layer on baking sheet.

3 Roast 15 to 18 minutes or until mushrooms are tender and browned.

Tip

Serve roasted mushrooms as a side dish with chicken or beef, or use them as a filling for sandwiches, tacos or quesadillas.

Summer Squash Skillet

—————— makes 4 servings ——————

2 tablespoons butter

1 medium sweet or yellow onion, thinly sliced and separated into rings

2 medium yellow squash or zucchini *or* 1 of each, sliced

¾ teaspoon salt

¼ teaspoon black pepper

1 large tomato, chopped

¼ cup chopped fresh basil

2 tablespoons grated Parmesan cheese

1 Melt butter in large skillet over medium-high heat. Add onion; stir to coat with butter. Cover and cook 3 minutes. Reduce heat to medium; cook, uncovered, 3 minutes or until onion is golden brown.

2 Add squash, salt and pepper; cover and cook 5 minutes, stirring once. Add tomato; cook, uncovered, 2 minutes or until squash is tender. Stir in basil; sprinkle with cheese.

Charred Corn and Black Beans

— makes 6 servings —

3 tablespoons lime juice

½ teaspoon salt

¼ cup extra virgin olive oil

4 to 5 ears corn, husked (enough to make 3 cups kernels)

1 cup canned black beans, rinsed and drained

½ cup chopped fresh cilantro

2 teaspoons minced seeded chipotle pepper (about 1 canned chipotle pepper in adobo sauce)

1 Whisk lime juice and salt in small bowl. Gradually whisk in oil until well blended; set aside.

2 Cut corn kernels off cobs. Heat large skillet over medium-high heat. Cook corn in single layer 15 to 17 minutes or until browned and tender, stirring frequently. Transfer to large bowl to cool slightly.

3 Place beans in small microwavable bowl; microwave on HIGH 1 minute or until heated through. Add beans, cilantro and chipotle pepper to corn; mix well. Pour lime juice mixture over corn mixture; stir gently to coat.

Tip

Store leftover chipotle peppers in adobo sauce in a covered food storage container in the refrigerator or freezer.

Kale with Lemon and Garlic

———— makes 8 servings ————

2 bunches kale or Swiss chard
(1 to 1¼ pounds)

1 tablespoon olive oil

3 cloves garlic, minced

½ cup chicken or vegetable broth

½ teaspoon salt

¼ teaspoon black pepper

1 lemon, cut into 8 wedges

1 Trim any tough stems from kale. Stack and thinly slice leaves.

2 Heat oil in large saucepan over medium heat. Add garlic; cook 3 minutes, stirring occasionally. Add chopped kale and broth; cover and simmer 7 minutes. Stir kale; cover and cook over medium-low heat 8 to 10 minutes or until kale is tender.

3 Stir in salt and pepper. Squeeze wedge of lemon over each serving.

Bountiful Bowls

Pepper and Egg Couscous Bowl

— makes 4 servings —

1 tablespoon olive oil

3 red and yellow bell peppers, cut into ¼-inch strips

1 red onion, cut in half and thinly sliced

2 cups vegetable broth

1 cup uncooked couscous

1 clove garlic, minced

½ teaspoon salt

½ teaspoon dried oregano

½ teaspoon ground cumin

4 to 8 eggs, cooked any style

1 can (about 15 ounces) black beans, rinsed and drained

1 cup grape tomatoes, halved

Crumbled queso fresco, cotija or feta cheese (optional)

1 Heat oil in large skillet over medium-high heat. Add bell peppers and onion; cook and stir 5 minutes or until vegetables are tender.

2 Bring broth to a boil in small saucepan over high heat. Stir in couscous, garlic, salt, oregano and cumin. Remove from heat; cover and let stand 5 minutes. Fluff with fork.

3 Divide couscous amoung four bowls; top with vegetables, eggs, beans, tomatoes and cheese, if desired.

Shrimp and Soba Noodle Bowl

— makes 4 servings —

4 ounces soba noodles*

1 tablespoon vegetable oil

2 cups diagonally sliced green beans (bite-size pieces)

1½ cups sliced mushrooms

2 tablespoons orange juice

2 tablespoons lime juice

1 tablespoon soy sauce

2 teaspoons dark sesame oil

1½ cups (6 ounces) cooked medium shrimp (with tails on)

¼ cup thinly sliced red bell pepper

2 tablespoons finely chopped fresh cilantro

1 to 2 tablespoons toasted sesame seeds (optional)

Soba is a Japanese noodle made from buckwheat flour. If unavailable, substitute linguine and cook according to package directions.

1 Cook noodles according to package directions; drain and rinse under warm water. Drain again; transfer to large bowl.

2 Heat vegetable oil in large skillet over medium-high heat. Add green beans and mushrooms; cook 8 minutes or until mushrooms are lightly browned and beans are softened, stirring occasionally.

3 Meanwhile, whisk orange juice, lime juice, soy sauce and sesame oil in small bowl until well blended.

4 Combine noodles, shrimp, green bean mixture and bell pepper in large bowl. Pour dressing over salad; sprinkle with cilantro and sesame seeds, if desired. Toss gently to coat.

Turkey Taco Bowls

—— makes 4 servings ——

1 pound ground turkey

1 package (1 ounce) taco seasoning mix

¾ cup water

1 package (10 ounces) frozen cauliflower rice

2 cups shredded red cabbage

2 green onions, finely chopped

1 avocado, thinly sliced

2 plum tomatoes, diced

Optional toppings: minced fresh cilantro, sour cream and crumbled cotija cheese

1 Cook turkey in large nonstick skillet over medium-high heat 6 to 8 minutes or until no longer pink, stirring to break up meat.

2 Stir in taco seasoning mix and water; bring to a boil. Reduce heat to medium-low; cook 5 minutes, stirring occasionally.

3 Heat cauliflower rice according to package directions. Divide among four bowls; top with turkey, cabbage, green onions, avocado and tomatoes. Serve with desired toppings.

Quinoa Burrito Bowls

—————— makes 4 servings ——————

1 cup uncooked quinoa

2 cups water

2 tablespoons lime juice, divided

2 teaspoons vegetable oil

1 small onion, diced

1 red bell pepper, diced

1 clove garlic, minced

½ cup canned black beans, rinsed and drained

½ cup thawed frozen corn

¼ cup sour cream

Shredded lettuce

Lime wedges (optional)

1 Place quinoa in fine-mesh strainer; rinse well under cold water. Bring 2 cups water to a boil in small saucepan; stir in quinoa. Reduce heat to low; cover and simmer 10 to 15 minutes or until quinoa is tender and water is absorbed. Stir in 1 tablespoon lime juice. Cover and keep warm.

2 Meanwhile, heat oil in large skillet over medium heat. Add onion and bell pepper; cook and stir 5 minutes or until softened. Add garlic; cook and stir 1 minute. Add black beans and corn; cook 3 to 5 minutes or until heated through, stirring occasioally.

3 Combine sour cream and remaining 1 tablespoon lime juice in small bowl; mix well.

4 Divide quinoa among four bowls; top with black bean mixture, lettuce and sour cream mixture. Garnish with lime wedges.

Bowtie Pasta Bowl

—————— makes 4 servings ——————

3 cups chicken broth

6 ounces uncooked bowtie pasta

⅛ teaspoon red pepper flakes

1½ cups diced cooked chicken

1 medium tomato, seeded and diced

1 cup packed spring greens or spinach, coarsely chopped

3 tablespoons chopped fresh basil

½ teaspoon salt

1 cup (4 ounces) shredded mozzarella cheese

2 tablespoons grated Parmesan cheese

1 Bring broth to boil in large saucepan over high heat. Add pasta and red pepper flakes; return to a boil. Reduce heat to low; cover and cook 10 minutes or until pasta is al dente.

2 Add chicken; cook 1 minute. Remove from heat; stir in tomato, greens, basil and salt.

3 Spoon pasta mixture into four shallow bowls; top with mozzarella and Parmesan cheeses.

Green Curry with Tofu

———————— makes 2 servings ————————

1 tablespoon vegetable oil

1 onion, chopped

1 package (14 ounces) firm tofu, drained and cut into 1-inch cubes

⅓ cup Thai green curry paste

1 can (about 13 ounces) coconut milk

1 broccoli crown (about 8 ounces), cut into florets

1 cup cut green beans (1-inch pieces)

½ teaspoon salt

Hot cooked brown rice or rice noodles

1 Heat oil in large skillet over high heat. Add onion; cook and stir 5 minutes or until lightly browned.

2 Add tofu and curry paste; cook and stir 2 minutes or until curry is fragrant and tofu is coated. Add coconut milk; bring to a boil. Reduce heat to low; stir in broccoli and green beans.

3 Cook 20 minutes or until vegetables are tender and sauce is thickened, stirring frequently. Season with salt. Serve over rice.

Lemon Broccoli Pasta Bowl

—————— makes 2 servings ——————

1 tablespoon olive oil

3 tablespoons sliced green onions

1 clove garlic, minced

2 cups chicken broth

1½ teaspoons grated lemon peel

⅛ teaspoon black pepper

2 cups fresh or frozen broccoli florets

3 ounces uncooked angel hair pasta

⅓ cup sour cream

2 tablespoons grated Parmesan cheese

1 Heat oil in large saucepan over medium heat. Add green onions and garlic; cook and stir 3 minutes or until green onions are tender.

2 Stir in broth, lemon peel and pepper; bring to a boil over high heat. Stir in broccoli and pasta; return to a boil. Reduce heat to low; cook 6 to 7 minutes or until pasta is tender, stirring frequently.

3 Remove from heat; stir in sour cream until well blended. Let stand 5 minutes. Top with cheese.

Spicy Tuna Sushi Bowl

—————— makes 2 servings ——————

2 tablespoons mayonnaise

1 teaspoon sriracha or hot pepper sauce

3 teaspoons unseasoned rice wine vinegar, divided

1 tuna steak (about 6 ounces)

1 cup hot cooked brown rice

¼ cup diced cucumber

¼ ripe avocado, sliced

Black sesame seeds (optional)

1 Whisk mayonnaise, sriracha and 1 teaspoon vinegar in small bowl until well blended. Rub tuna evenly with half of sauce. Marinate 10 minutes.

2 Meanwhile, stir remaining 2 teaspoons vinegar into rice in small bowl; set aside.

3 Heat small nonstick skillet over medium-high heat. Add tuna; cook 2 minutes per side for medium-rare or to desired doneness. Slice tuna.

4 Divide rice between two bowls; top with cucumber, avocado and tuna. Sprinkle with sesame seeds, if desired. Serve with remaining half of sauce.

Salsa Salad Bowl

———— makes 4 servings ————

1 can (about 15 ounces) black beans, rinsed and drained

1 pint grape or cherry tomatoes, quartered

4 ounces mozzarella cheese, cut into ¼-inch cubes

½ medium poblano or green bell pepper, chopped

½ cup chopped red onion

⅓ cup chopped fresh cilantro

¼ cup lime juice (juice of 2 medium limes)

2 tablespoons extra virgin olive oil

½ teaspoon salt

⅛ teaspoon ground red pepper

1 Combine beans, tomatoes, cheese, poblano pepper, onion and cilantro in medium bowl; mix well.

2 Whisk lime juice, oil, salt and red pepper in small bowl until well blended.

3 Pour dressing over salad; stir gently to coat.

Shanghai Pork Noodle Bowl

— makes 4 servings —

8 ounces uncooked whole wheat spaghetti, broken in half

⅓ cup reduced-sodium teriyaki sauce

2 tablespoons rice vinegar

¼ teaspoon red pepper flakes

4 teaspoons vegetable oil, divided

1 pound pork tenderloin, halved lengthwise and cut into ¼-inch slices

4 cups sliced bok choy

1 can (11 ounces) mandarin orange sections, drained

½ cup sliced green onions

1 Cook noodles according to package directions; drain and keep warm in large bowl. Whisk teriyaki sauce, vinegar and red pepper flakes in small bowl until well blended. Set aside.

2 Heat 2 teaspoons oil in large nonstick skillet over medium-high heat. Add half of pork to skillet; stir-fry 2 to 3 minutes or until pork is barely pink. Remove to plate. Repeat with remaining 2 teaspoons oil and half of pork.

3 Add bok choy to skillet; stir-fry 1 to 2 minutes or until wilted. Return pork to skillet with teriyaki mixture; cook and stir until heated through.

4 Add pork mixture, orange sections and green onions to noodles; toss to coat.

Tofu "Fried" Rice Bowl

———— makes 1 serving ————

2 ounces extra firm tofu

¼ cup finely chopped broccoli

¼ cup thawed frozen shelled
edamame

⅓ cup cooked brown rice

1 tablespoon chopped green onion

½ teaspoon soy sauce

⅛ teaspoon garlic powder

⅛ teaspoon sesame oil

⅛ teaspoon sriracha or hot
pepper sauce (optional)

1 Press tofu between paper towels to remove excess water. Cut into ½-inch cubes.

2 Combine tofu, broccoli and edamame in large microwavable mug or bowl; mix well.
Microwave on HIGH 1 minute.

3 Stir in rice, green onion, soy sauce, garlic powder, oil and sriracha, if desired. Microwave
1 minute or until heated through. Stir well before serving.

One-Pot Pasta

—— makes 4 servings ——

6 ounces uncooked rotini pasta

1 can (about 15 ounces) navy beans

8 ounces grape tomatoes, halved

3 cups packed fresh spinach (3 ounces), coarsely chopped

5 slices hard salami (2 ounces), cut into very thin strips

20 kalamata olives, pitted and coarsely chopped

⅓ to ½ cup olive oil vinaigrette

3 to 4 tablespoons chopped fresh basil

4 ounces crumbled feta cheese with basil and sun-dried tomatoes

1 Cook pasta in large saucepan of boiling salted water according to package directions for al dente.

2 Meanwhile, drain beans and tomatoes in colander. Drain cooked pasta into beans and tomatoes; shake off excess liquid.

3 Return pasta mixture to saucepan. Add spinach, salami, olives, ⅓ cup vinaigrette and basil; toss gently to coat. (Heat will wilt spinach slightly.) Top with cheese; toss again. Add additional vinaigrette if salad seems dry. Cover and let stand 5 minutes before serving.

Note

Refrigerate leftovers to eat as a salad the next day; add additional dressing to taste.

Quick Skillets

Pork and Asparagus Stir-Fry

—————————— makes 4 servings ——————————

1 tablespoon vegetable oil

12 ounces pork tenderloin,
   cut into bite-size pieces

3 tablespoons Chinese
   black bean sauce

½ teaspoon black pepper

12 ounces asparagus (25 to
   30 spears, cut diagonally
   into 1-inch pieces)

2 to 3 tablespoons water

   Hot cooked rice (optional)

1 Heat oil in large skillet over medium-high heat. Add pork, black bean sauce and pepper; stir-fry 5 minutes or until pork is browned.

2 Add asparagus and water to skillet; stir-fry until pork is cooked through and asparagus is crisp-tender, adding additional water if needed to prevent sticking. Serve over rice, if desired.

Mexican Cauliflower and Bean Skillet

—— makes 4 to 6 servings ——

1 tablespoon olive oil

3 cups coarsely chopped
   cauliflower

¾ teaspoon salt

½ medium onion, chopped

1 green bell pepper, chopped

1 clove garlic, minced

1 teaspoon chili powder

¾ teaspoon ground cumin

   Pinch ground red pepper

1 can (about 15 ounces) black
   beans, rinsed and drained

1 cup (4 ounces) shredded
   Cheddar-Jack cheese

   Salsa and sour cream

1 Heat oil in large nonstick skillet over medium-high heat. Add cauliflower and salt;
cook and stir 5 minutes. Add onion, bell pepper, garlic, chili powder, cumin and
ground red pepper; cook and stir 5 minutes or until cauliflower is tender.

2 Stir in beans; cook until beans are heated through. Remove from heat.

3 Sprinkle with cheese; fold in gently and let stand until cheese is melted. Serve
with salsa and sour cream.

Serving Suggestion

Serve over brown rice or with warm corn tortillas.

Seared Scallops with Garlic-Lemon Spinach

———————— makes 4 servings ————————

1 tablespoon olive oil

1 pound sea scallops* (about 12)

¼ teaspoon salt

⅛ teaspoon black pepper

2 cloves garlic, minced

1 shallot, minced

1 package (6 ounces) baby spinach

1 tablespoon lemon juice

Lemon wedges (optional)

Make sure scallops are dry before putting them in the skillet so they can get a golden crust.

1 Heat oil in large nonstick skillet over medium-high heat. Add scallops; sprinkle with salt and pepper. Cook 2 to 3 minutes per side or until golden brown. Remove to large plate; tent with foil to keep warm.

2 Add garlic and shallot to skillet; cook and stir 45 seconds or until fragrant. Add spinach; cook 2 minutes or until spinach just begins to wilt, stirring occasionally. Remove from heat; stir in lemon juice.

3 Serve scallops over spinach. Garnish with lemon wedges.

Curried Noodles

—— makes 4 servings ——

7 ounces thin rice noodles (rice vermicelli)

1 tablespoon peanut or vegetable oil

1 large red bell pepper, cut into short, thin strips

2 green onions, cut into ½-inch pieces

1 clove garlic, minced

1 teaspoon minced fresh ginger

2 teaspoons curry powder

⅛ to ¼ teaspoon red pepper flakes

½ cup chicken broth

2 tablespoons soy sauce

1 Place noodles in large bowl; cover with boiling water. Soak 15 minutes to soften. Drain well; cut into 3-inch pieces.

2 Heat oil in large skillet over medium-high heat. Add bell pepper; cook and stir 3 minutes. Add green onions, garlic and ginger; cook and stir 1 minute. Add curry powder and red pepper flakes; cook and stir 1 minute.

3 Stir in broth and soy sauce; cook 2 minutes. Add noodles; cook and stir 3 minutes or until heated through.

Chicken and Vegetable Fajitas

—————————————— makes 6 servings ——————————————

1 pound boneless skinless chicken thighs, cut crosswise into strips

1 teaspoon dried oregano

1 teaspoon chili powder

½ teaspoon garlic salt

1 tablespoon vegetable oil

2 bell peppers, cut into thin strips

4 thin slices large onion, separated into rings

½ cup salsa

6 (6-inch) flour tortillas, warmed

½ cup chopped fresh cilantro or green onions

Sour cream (optional)

1 Combine chicken, oregano, chili powder and garlic salt in medium bowl; toss to coat.

2 Heat oil in large skillet over medium-high heat. Add chicken; cook and stir 5 to 6 minutes or until cooked through. Remove to plate.

3 Add bell peppers and onion to skillet; cook and stir 2 minutes over medium heat. Add salsa; cover and cook 6 to 8 minutes or until vegetables are tender.

4 Return chicken to skillet; cook, uncovered, 2 minutes or until heated through. Serve with tortillas; top with cilantro and sour cream, if desired.

Tex-Mex Black Bean and Corn Stew

———————————— makes 4 servings ————————————

1 tablespoon vegetable oil

1 small onion, chopped

4 cloves garlic, minced

1 teaspoon chili powder

1 teaspoon ground cumin

1 can (about 14 ounces) fire-roasted diced tomatoes

¾ cup salsa

2 medium zucchini or yellow squash (or 1 of each), cut into ½-inch pieces

1 can (about 15 ounces) black beans, rinsed and drained

1 cup frozen corn

½ cup (2 ounces) shredded Cheddar or pepper jack cheese

¼ cup chopped fresh cilantro or green onion

1 Heat oil in large skillet over medium heat. Add onion; cook and stir 5 minutes. Add garlic, chili powder and cumin; cook and stir 1 minute.

2 Stir in tomatoes, salsa, zucchini, beans and corn; bring to a boil over high heat. Reduce heat to low; cover and simmer 20 minutes or until vegetables are tender. Top with cheese and cilantro.

Hoisin Chicken and Broccoli Stir-Fry

—————————————— makes 4 servings ——————————————

2 teaspoons dark sesame oil

1 pound boneless skinless chicken
    thighs, cut into short, thin
    strips

4 cloves garlic, minced

¼ teaspoon red pepper flakes

1 large red bell pepper, cut into
    short, thin strips

2 cups broccoli florets

1 cup matchstick carrots or
    grated carrots

2 tablespoons light soy sauce

2 teaspoons cornstarch

2 tablespoons hoisin sauce

Hot cooked rice (optional)

1 Heat oil in large skillet over medium-high heat. Add chicken, garlic and red pepper flakes; stir-fry 1 minute.

2 Add bell pepper, broccoli and carrots; stir-fry over medium heat 5 to 6 minutes or until chicken is cooked through and vegetables are crisp-tender.

3 Stir soy sauce into cornstarch in small bowl until smooth. Add to skillet with hoisin sauce; cook and stir 1 to 2 minutes or until sauce thickens. Serve over rice, if desired.

——————————————— *Tip* ———————————————
To save time, look for packages of fully cooked rice at the supermarket.
Each package (about 8 ounces) contains 2 cups cooked rice which can
be heated quickly in the microwave.

Shrimp and Veggie Skillet

———————— makes 4 servings ————————

¼ cup soy sauce

2 tablespoons lime juice

1 tablespoon sesame oil

1 teaspoon grated fresh ginger

⅛ teaspoon red pepper flakes

4 teaspoons vegetable oil, divided

8 ounces medium raw shrimp (about 32), peeled and deveined (with tails on)

2 medium zucchini, cut in half lengthwise and thinly sliced

6 green onions, trimmed and halved lengthwise

1 cup grape tomatoes

1 Whisk soy sauce, lime juice, oil, ginger and red pepper flakes in small bowl until well blended.

2 Heat 2 teaspoons oil in large nonstick skillet over medium-high heat. Add shrimp; cook and stir 3 minutes or until shrimp are opaque. Remove to large bowl.

3 Add remaining 2 teaspoons oil to skillet; heat over medium-high heat. Add zucchini; cook and stir 4 to 6 minutes or just until crisp-tender. Add green onions and tomatoes; cook 2 minutes. Return shrimp to skillet, cook 1 minute. Transfer to large bowl.

4 Add soy sauce mixture to skillet; bring to a boil, scraping up browned bits from bottom of skillet. Remove from heat; stir in shrimp and vegetables. Stir gently to coat.

Quick Vegetable Quesadillas

———————————— makes 4 servings ————————————

1 tablespoon olive oil

1 small zucchini, chopped

½ cup chopped onion

½ cup chopped green bell pepper

2 cloves garlic, minced

½ teaspoon chili powder

½ teaspoon ground cumin

8 (6-inch) flour tortillas

1 cup (4 ounces) shredded Cheddar cheese

¼ cup chopped fresh cilantro

1 Heat oil in large skillet over medium heat. Add zucchini, onion, bell pepper, garlic, chili powder and cumin; cook and stir 3 to 4 minutes or until vegetables are crisp-tender.

2 Spoon vegetable mixture evenly over half of each tortilla; sprinkle with cheese and cilantro. Fold each tortilla in half.

3 Wipe out skillet with paper towel; spray with nonstick cooking spray. Add quesadillas to skillet in batches; cook over medium heat 2 minutes per side or until lightly browned.

Sassy Chicken and Peppers

— makes 4 servings —

1 tablespoon Mexican seasoning*

4 boneless skinless chicken breasts
(about ¼ pound each)

1 tablespoon vegetable oil

1 red onion, sliced

1 medium red bell pepper,
cut into thin strips

1 medium yellow or green bell
pepper, cut into thin strips

½ cup chunky salsa or chipotle
salsa

2 tablespoons lime juice

Lime wedges (optional)

*If Mexican seasoning is not available,
substitute 1 teaspoon chili powder,
½ teaspoon ground cumin, ½ teaspoon
salt and ⅛ teaspoon ground red pepper.*

1 Sprinkle Mexican seasoning over both sides of chicken.

2 Heat oil in large nonstick skillet over medium heat. Add onion; cook 3 minutes, stirring occasionally. Add bell peppers; cook 3 minutes, stirring occasionally. Stir in salsa and lime juice.

3 Push vegetables to edge of skillet. Add chicken to skillet; cook 5 minutes. Turn and cook 4 minutes or until chicken is no longer pink in center and vegetables are tender.

4 Serve chicken over vegetables. Garnish with lime wedges.

Spicy Chinese Pepper Steak

———————— makes 4 servings ————————

1 boneless beef top sirloin steak (about 1 pound) or tenderloin tips, cut into thin strips

1 tablespoon cornstarch

3 cloves garlic, minced

½ teaspoon red pepper flakes

2 tablespoons peanut or canola oil, divided

1 green bell pepper, cut into thin strips

1 red bell pepper, cut into thin strips

¼ cup oyster sauce

2 tablespoons soy sauce

3 tablespoons chopped fresh cilantro or green onions

1 Combine beef, cornstarch, garlic and red pepper flakes in medium bowl; toss to coat.

2 Heat 1 tablespoon oil in large skillet over medium-high heat. Add bell peppers; cook and stir 3 minutes. Remove to small bowl. Add remaining 1 tablespoon oil and beef mixture to skillet; cook and stir 4 to 5 minutes or until beef is barely pink in center.

3 Add oyster sauce and soy sauce to skillet; cook and stir 1 minute. Return bell peppers to skillet; cook and stir 1 to 2 minutes or until sauce thickens. Sprinkle with cilantro.

Curry Tofu and Vegetables

———— makes 4 servings ————

1 package (about 14 ounces)
   extra firm tofu, cut into
   ¾-inch cubes

¾ cup coconut milk

2 tablespoons lime juice

1 tablespoon curry powder

2 teaspoons dark sesame oil,
   divided

4 cups broccoli florets
   (1½-inch pieces)

2 medium red bell peppers,
   cut into short, thin strips

1 medium red onion, cut into
   thin wedges

½ teaspoon salt

   Hot cooked brown rice (optional)

1 Press tofu cubes between layers of paper towels to remove excess moisture. Combine coconut milk, lime juice and curry powder in medium bowl; mix well.

2 Heat 1 teaspoon oil in large nonstick skillet over medium heat. Add tofu; cook 10 minutes or until lightly browned on all sides, turning occasionally. Remove to plate.

3 Add remaining 1 teaspoon oil to skillet. Add broccoli, bell peppers and onion; cook and stir over high heat about 5 minutes or until vegetables are crisp-tender. Return tofu to skillet with coconut milk mixture; bring to a boil, stirring frequently. Stir in salt. Serve immediately with rice, if desired.

Southwestern Chicken and Black Bean Skillet

—————— makes 4 servings ——————

1 teaspoon ground cumin

1 teaspoon chili powder

½ teaspoon salt

4 boneless skinless chicken breasts (about 1 pound)

1 tablespoon vegetable oil

1 cup chopped onion

1 red bell pepper, chopped

1 can (about 15 ounces) black beans, rinsed and drained

½ cup chunky salsa

Lime wedges (optional)

¼ cup chopped fresh cilantro or green onions (optional)

1 Combine cumin, chili powder and salt in small bowl; sprinkle evenly over both sides of chicken.

2 Heat oil in large skillet over medium-high heat. Add chicken; cook 2 minutes per side. Remove to plate.

3 Add onion to skillet; cook and stir 1 minute. Add bell pepper; cook 5 minutes, stirring occasionally. Stir in beans and salsa.

4 Place chicken on top of bean mixture; cover and cook 6 to 7 minutes or until chicken is no longer pink in center. Serve with lime wedges and top with cilantro, if desired.

Easy Entrées

Lemon-Garlic Salmon with Tzatziki Sauce

makes 4 servings

½ cup diced cucumber

¾ teaspoon salt, divided

1 cup plain Greek yogurt

2 tablespoons lemon juice, divided

1 teaspoon grated lemon peel, divided

1 teaspoon minced garlic, divided

¼ teaspoon black pepper

4 skinless salmon fillets (4 ounces each)

1 Place cucumber in small colander set over small bowl; sprinkle with ¼ teaspoon salt. Drain 1 hour.

2 For tzatziki sauce, combine yogurt, cucumber, 1 tablespoon lemon juice, ½ teaspoon lemon peel, ½ teaspoon garlic and ¼ teaspoon salt in small bowl; mix well. Cover and refrigerate until ready to use.

3 Combine remaining 1 tablespoon lemon juice, ½ teaspoon lemon peel, ½ teaspoon garlic, ¼ teaspoon salt and pepper in small bowl; mix well. Rub evenly over salmon.

4 Heat nonstick grill pan over medium-high heat. Cook salmon 5 minutes per side or until fish begins to flake when tested with fork. Serve with tzatziki sauce.

Szechuan Cold Noodles

—————— makes 4 servings ——————

8 ounces uncooked vermicelli, broken in half, or Chinese egg noodles

3 tablespoons rice vinegar

3 tablespoons soy sauce

2 tablespoons peanut or vegetable oil

1 clove garlic, minced

1 teaspoon minced fresh ginger

1 teaspoon dark sesame oil

½ teaspoon crushed Szechuan peppercorns or red pepper flakes

¼ cup coarsely chopped fresh cilantro (optional)

¼ cup chopped peanuts

1 Cook noodles according to package directions; drain.

2 Combine vinegar, soy sauce, peanut oil, garlic, ginger, sesame oil and peppercorns in large bowl; mix well.

3 Add hot cooked noodles to sauce; toss to coat. Sprinkle with cilantro, if desired, and peanuts. Serve at room temperature or chilled.

—————— *Szechuan Vegetable Noodles* ——————

Stir in 1 cup chopped peeled cucumber, ½ cup chopped red bell pepper, ½ cup sliced green onions and an additional 1 tablespoon soy sauce.

Grilled Pork Fajitas

makes 4 servings

2 cloves garlic, minced

2 teaspoons chili powder

½ teaspoon ground cumin

½ teaspoon ground coriander

12 ounces pork tenderloin

1 medium red onion, cut into ½-inch slices

1 mango, peeled and cut into ½-inch pieces

8 (6-inch) flour tortillas, warmed

½ cup salsa verde

1 Spray grid with nonstick cooking spray. Prepare grill for direct cooking.

2 Combine garlic, chili powder, cumin and coriander in small bowl; mix well. Rub spice mixture all over pork.

3 Grill over medium-high heat 12 to 16 minutes or until pork is 145°F, turning occasionally. Add onion to grill during last 8 minutes of cooking; grill until tender, turning occasionally.

4 Remove onion to small bowl. Remove pork to cutting board; tent loosely with foil and let stand 5 to 10 minutes.

5 Cut pork into ½-inch strips Serve pork, onion and mango in tortillas; top with salsa verde.

Pasta with Tuna, Green Beans and Tomatoes

—— makes 4 servings ——

8 ounces uncooked whole wheat penne, rigatoni or fusilli pasta

1½ cups frozen cut green beans

2 tablespoons olive oil, divided

3 green onions, sliced

1 clove garlic, minced

1 can (about 14 ounces) diced Italian-style tomatoes, drained

½ teaspoon salt

½ teaspoon Italian seasoning

¼ teaspoon black pepper

1 can (12 ounces) solid albacore tuna packed in water, drained and flaked

Chopped fresh parsley (optional)

1 Cook pasta according to package directions, adding green beans during last 7 minutes of cooking time. (Allow water to return to a boil before resuming timing.) Drain and keep warm.

2 Meanwhile, heat 1 tablespoon oil in large skillet over medium heat. Add green onions and garlic; cook and stir 2 minutes. Add tomatoes, salt, Italian seasoning and pepper; cook and stir 4 to 5 minutes.

3 Add pasta and beans, tuna and remaining 1 tablespoon oil to skillet; mix gently. Sprinkle with parsley, if desired. Serve immediately.

Grilled Fish Tacos

makes 4 servings

¾ teaspoon chili powder

1 pound skinless mahi mahi, halibut or tilapia fillets

½ cup salsa, divided

2 cups packaged coleslaw mix or cabbage

¼ cup sour cream

4 tablespoons chopped fresh cilantro, divided

8 (6-inch) corn tortillas, warmed

1 Prepare grill for direct cooking. Sprinkle chili powder over mahi mahi. Spoon ¼ cup salsa over fish; let stand 10 minutes.

2 Meanwhile, combine coleslaw mix, remaining ¼ cup salsa, sour cream and 2 tablespoons cilantro in large bowl; mix well.

3 Grill mahi mahi, salsa side up, covered, over medium heat 8 to 10 minutes or until fish is opaque in center and begins to flake when tested with fork.

4 Slice mahi mahi crosswise into thin strips or break into chunks. Fill warm tortillas with fish and coleslaw mixture; top with remaining 2 tablespoons cilantro.

Peanut-Sauced Pasta

—— makes 4 servings ——

⅓ cup vegetable broth

3 tablespoons creamy peanut butter

2 tablespoons seasoned rice vinegar

2 tablespoons soy sauce

½ teaspoon red pepper flakes

9 ounces uncooked multigrain linguine

1½ pounds fresh asparagus, cut into 1-inch pieces (4 cups)

⅓ cup dry-roasted peanuts, chopped

1 Whisk broth, peanut butter, vinegar, soy sauce and red pepper flakes in small saucepan until smooth. Cook over low heat until heated through, stirring frequently. Keep warm.

2 Cook pasta in large saucepan of boiling salted water according to package directions, adding asparagus to saucepan during last 5 minutes of cooking.

3 Drain pasta and asparagus; return to saucepan. Add peanut sauce; toss to coat. Sprinkle with peanuts.

Pan-Seared Halibut with Avocado Salsa

—————— makes 4 servings ——————

4 tablespoons chipotle salsa, divided

½ teaspoon salt, divided

4 small (4 to 5 ounces each) *or* 2 large (8 to 10 ounces each) halibut steaks, cut ¾ inch thick

2 teaspoons vegetable oil

½ cup diced tomato

½ ripe avocado, diced

2 tablespoons chopped fresh cilantro (optional)

Lime wedges (optional)

1 Combine 2 tablespoons salsa and ¼ teaspoon salt in small bowl; spread over both sides of halibut.

2 Heat oil in large nonstick skillet over medium heat. Add halibut; cook 4 to 5 minutes per side or until fish is opaque in center.

3 Meanwhile, combine remaining 2 tablespoons salsa, ¼ teaspoon salt, tomato, avocado and cilantro, if desired, in small bowl; mix well.

4 Spoon salsa over halibut. Serve with lime wedges, if desired.

Pesto Pasta with Asparagus and Tomatoes

makes 4 servings

8 ounces uncooked thin spaghetti

8 ounces fresh asparagus, cut into 2-inch pieces

1 medium tomato, chopped

1 jar (3½ ounces) pesto

2 tablespoons extra virgin olive oil

1 clove garlic, minced

½ teaspoon black pepper

¼ cup shredded Parmesan cheese

1 Cook pasta in large saucepan of boiling salted water according to package directions, adding asparagus to saucepan during last 3 minutes of cooking.

2 Meanwhile, combine tomato, pesto, oil, garlic and pepper in large bowl; mix well.

3 Drain pasta and asparagus. Add to bowl with pesto mixture; toss gently to coat. Sprinkle with cheese.

Salmon with Dill-Mustard Sauce

———————————— makes 4 servings ————————————

2 tablespoons lemon juice

2 tablespoons lime juice

4 salmon fillets (4 ounces each)

¼ cup mayonnaise

1 tablespoon Dijon mustard

1 tablespoon chopped fresh dill sprigs, plus additional for garnish

1 Combine lemon juice and lime juice in glass baking dish. Rinse salmon and pat dry. Place salmon in baking dish; turn to coat. Marinate 10 minutes, turning once.

2 Combine mayonnaise, mustard and 1 tablespoon dill in small bowl; mix well.

3 Preheat broiler. Spray rack of broiler pan with nonstick cooking spray. Remove salmon from marinade; pat dry. Place on prepared rack.

4 Broil 4 inches from heat source 3 to 4 minutes per side or until fish begins to flake when tested with fork. Spoon sauce over salmon; sprinkle with additional dill.

Penne with Chunky Spinach Tomato Sauce

—————— makes 6 servings ——————

8 ounces uncooked multigrain penne pasta

2 cups spicy marinara sauce

1 large ripe tomato, chopped (about 1½ cups)

4 cups packed baby spinach or torn spinach leaves (4 ounces)

¼ cup grated Parmesan cheese

¼ cup chopped fresh basil

1 Cook pasta according to package directions.

2 Meanwhile, heat marinara sauce and tomato in medium saucepan over medium heat 3 to 4 minutes or until hot and bubbly, stirring occasionally. Remove from heat; stir in spinach.

3 Drain pasta; return to saucepan. Add sauce; stir to coat. Top with cheese and basil.

Adriatic-Style Halibut

—— makes 4 servings ——

1 large tomato, seeded and diced (about 1¼ cups)

⅓ cup coarsely sliced pitted kalamata olives

1 clove garlic, minced

4 skinless halibut or red snapper fillets (about 6 ounces each)

¾ teaspoon coarse salt

¼ teaspoon black pepper

1 tablespoon olive oil

¼ cup dry white wine or vermouth

Fresh basil or Italian parsley sprigs (optional)

1 Preheat oven to 200°F. Combine tomato, olives and garlic in small bowl; mix well.

2 Season halibut with ¾ teaspoon salt and ¼ teaspoon pepper. Heat oil in large nonstick skillet over medium heat. Add halibut; cook 4 to 5 minutes per side or until fish is opaque in center. Transfer to serving platter or plate; keep warm in oven.

3 Add wine to skillet; cook over high heat until reduced by half. Add tomato mixture; cook and stir 1 to 2 minutes or until heated through. Season with additional salt and pepper.

4 Spoon tomato mixture over halibut; garnish with basil.

Spaghetti Mediterranean

———— makes 4 servings ————

1½ pounds fresh tomatoes
  (about 4 large)

8 ounces uncooked spaghetti

¼ cup olive oil

2 cloves garlic, minced

½ cup chopped fresh parsley

12 pitted green olives, sliced

4 to 6 flat anchovy fillets, chopped

1 tablespoon drained capers

2 teaspoons chopped fresh basil
  or ½ teaspoon dried basil

½ teaspoon salt, plus additional
  for cooking pasta

½ teaspoon dried oregano

¼ teaspoon red pepper flakes

1 Bring large saucepan of water to a boil over medium-high heat. Add tomatoes; cook 60 seconds to loosen skins. Immediately remove tomatoes from saucepan (reserve water for cooking pasta) and rinse under cold water. Peel, seed and coarsely chop tomatoes.

2 Add salt to water in saucepan; return to a boil over medium-high heat. Cook spaghetti according to package directions for al dente; drain and keep warm.

3 Meanwhile, heat oil in large skillet over medium-high heat. Add garlic; cook 45 seconds or just until garlic begins to turn golden. Stir in tomatoes, parsley, olives, anchovies capers, basil, ½ teaspoon salt, oregano and red pepper flakes; cook 10 minutes or until most liquid has evaporated and sauce is slightly thickened, stirring occasionally.

4 Pour sauce over spaghetti; stir to coat. Serve immediately.

Index

Index

Index

Metric Conversion Chart

VOLUME MEASUREMENTS (dry)

⅛ teaspoon = 0.5 mL
¼ teaspoon = 1 mL
½ teaspoon = 2 mL
¾ teaspoon = 4 mL
1 teaspoon = 5 mL
1 tablespoon = 15 mL
2 tablespoons = 30 mL
¼ cup = 60 mL
⅓ cup = 75 mL
½ cup = 125 mL
⅔ cup = 150 mL
¾ cup = 175 mL
1 cup = 250 mL
2 cups = 1 pint = 500 mL
3 cups = 750 mL
4 cups = 1 quart = 1 L

VOLUME MEASUREMENTS (fluid)

1 fluid ounce (2 tablespoons) = 30 mL
4 fluid ounces (½ cup) = 125 mL
8 fluid ounces (1 cup) = 250 mL
12 fluid ounces (1½ cups) = 375 mL
16 fluid ounces (2 cups) = 500 mL

WEIGHTS (mass)

½ ounce = 15 g
1 ounce = 30 g
3 ounces = 90 g
4 ounces = 120 g
8 ounces = 225 g
10 ounces = 285 g
12 ounces = 360 g
16 ounces = 1 pound = 450 g

DIMENSIONS

1/16 inch = 2 mm
⅛ inch = 3 mm
¼ inch = 6 mm
½ inch = 1.5 cm
¾ inch = 2 cm
1 inch = 2.5 cm

OVEN TEMPERATURES

250°F = 120°C
275°F = 140°C
300°F = 150°C
325°F = 160°C
350°F = 180°C
375°F = 190°C
400°F = 200°C
425°F = 220°C
450°F = 230°C

BAKING PAN SIZES

Utensil	Size in Inches/Quarts	Metric Volume	Size in Centimeters
Baking or Cake Pan (square or rectangular)	8×8×2	2 L	20×20×5
	9×9×2	2.5 L	23×23×5
	12×8×2	3 L	30×20×5
	13×9×2	3.5 L	33×23×5
Loaf Pan	8×4×3	1.5 L	20×10×7
	9×5×3	2 L	23×13×7
Round Layer Cake Pan	8×1½	1.2 L	20×4
	9×1½	1.5 L	23×4
Pie Plate	8×1¼	750 mL	20×3
	9×1¼	1 L	23×3
Baking Dish or Casserole	1 quart	1 L	—
	1½ quart	1.5 L	—
	2 quart	2 L	—